Salvage

poems by

Cindy Milwe

Finishing Line Press
Georgetown, Kentucky

Salvage

Publisher: Leah Huete de Maines
Editor: Christen Kincaid
Cover Art: Whitney Scott, photograph "February, 2017"
Author Photo: Gene Reed, genereedphotography.com
Cover Design: Elizabeth Maines McCleavy

Order online: www.finishinglinepress.com
            also available on amazon.com

Author inquiries and mail orders:
Finishing Line Press
P. O. Box 1626
Georgetown, Kentucky 40324
U. S. A.

Table of Contents

In memory of my father

I'm a small stone, loose in the shale.
Love is my wound.

Theodore Roethke

Io

When Juno made me a cow,
I wept to my father who heard
only cow-sounds, not sorrow.

I didn't ask to be loved by such a god,
become soft animal alone in a pasture.
I knew my father could not help me.

Once made, girls are left on their own
to be taken and swallowed or changed
for the purpose of milking, of shame.

I.

Self-Examination

Mother's makeup mirror
between my young thighs,
I wanted to count each strand
one at a time, the first few
like daddy-longlegs' legs,
a spidery growth radiating
out from my center. I wanted
blood, boys, maybe even babies,
felt proud of my patch, my dark
surprise, secret. I couldn't wait
to be covered completely by fur,
hide the inner pink of a girl.

Miss Southern Connecticut

As the bathing suit competition ended—
bright lights in a conference room—

I felt wet and strange and left the row
of folding chairs for the Ladies' Room

at the Holiday Inn. In the stall,
I told myself the blood was a shit-stain,

but bunched wads of toilet paper
into my underwear—just in case.

My mother away, my friends onstage.
I didn't know what to do, stunned

by my worried reflection,
trying to feel beautiful.

Poker

They'd gather in our dining room
and cloud the house with cigar smoke—
Stanely Salzman, Leonard Liebman,
Rob Rosen, Paul Shulman,
Arthur Dinitz, Henry Bromberger,
Ron Melnick, and Sy Schmaholtz
who only had sons. On a silver tray,

I brought pastrami and pickles,
crumb cake and coffee, scotch
on the rocks when my father
was winning. Sy Schmaholtz
liked to chew the brown end of his stogie,
take a bite of his tongue sandwich,
and study me, shaking his bald head.
"Let me look at you, let me look
at you," he'd say, mouth full of flesh,
"Isn't she beautiful?" I tried hard

to serve, dressed up for good tips:
bra stuffed with tennis socks, fishnets
baggy at the ankles, a tiny pink skirt
that twirled when I spun. And when
they slipped their thick chips
into the pocket of my skirt, I liked
to finger them in the kitchen, feel
the gold at their center, stack them
and store them in neat little rows.

When I cashed in at midnight,
my mother would emerge in her bathrobe
and curlers, whisk me away with her jar
of cold cream. I'd return in pajamas
to kiss men goodnight as they left
for their lives. My mother and I cleaned up
in silence—wrapping brisket, folding card chairs,
picking cigarette butts from the rug.

Case History

Mother drank Tab,
never ate a sandwich
on two slices of bread,
cut grapefruit and carrots
for dinner. Still round
in control-top pantyhose,
her belly looked stuffed
in the nylon, meat packed
in its casing.
        My sister and I
used to stretch each other,
worked to lengthen our weight.
On the living room floor, we'd clamp
our toes under antique furniture,
raise our arms over our heads
toward the giant bay window
and pull.
        We dreamt
of other selves in other bodies,
drew stick-figure families in red
or green crayon, wished we had come
from another mother: willowy, tall.

Babysitting

I never wanted him to go to bed,
never wanted him to leave me alone
with the television and the parakeet
trapped behind bars and red velvet.

When he got tired, I took him upstairs
and curled up where he slept.
I read as many stories as he could take,
tickled his cheek as his eyes closed,
and kissed him goodnight
on his forehead, two times.

When his parents came home—
always late, glassy-eyed—
his father waited for me outside.
He drove me the mile to my house
in his smoke-filled Jaguar,
deep jazz in the eight-track.

Smiling, dazed, drunken—
he put ten dollars into my palm,
and watched from the driver's seat
as I closed our front door.

We never spoke in the car.
He was handsome; I was 13,
and Saturday nights got harder
each week: the boys, the men,
too old, too young.

Junior Bridesmaid

Fevered by strep,
it hurt to swallow
the crisp hors d'oeuvres.

I squeezed the cocktail napkin
to make things go down;
night beach air steamed.

When they exchanged vows
on my grandparents' splintery
dock—my Aunt Lizzy's thin

frame in dyed antique lace—
I felt guilt for the love
I felt for my new Uncle

Peter, the long-time
live-in, the "sin-in-law"
my Grandpa cherished.

How could I—in 7th grade,
having found spin-the-bottle
supremely disappointing—

be thinking of him as my husband?
I choked when they smashed
the glass and kissed, finally feeling

relieved to weep. There they were
in their life and here I was in mine.
I blubbered with my burning

throat, crammed hot crab cakes
into my mouth, chewed the briny,
deep-fried sea-flesh into pulp.

Tutoring with Mr. Dixon

So when he kissed me at the table
next to the box of donuts we shared,

I stopped caring about the math
he was teaching me for the crisp twenty

my mother laid out. I was more
than numbers. I wasn't afraid of his hands

on my neck, the way he looked into me
as if I had the answers.

Uneven

Half-girl, half-woman, one nipple
poked out of my chest like a sad eye
to see how the world had changed.

The other side stayed silent, stiff,
refusing to budge. Staunch girlhood—
right breast, right brain—it knew

its special task: holding on to the past.
It wanted its ponytails, swing sets,
ice skates and snowmen, boys

who just played their own tag.
The grown-up one stung, throbbed—
delayed reaction to my birth-slap.

I didn't know what I wanted—
for the tit to disappear or for God
to bring me its mate, lodged in the heart

of my chest-wall. Training bras helped—
folded squares under shirts in my bureau—
filled me out even as I grew more crooked

every year: fallen arches, lordotic spine,
knees that knocked in like arrows.
And like an arrow—unsteady and thin

in its quiver—I have never felt sturdy.
Though both breasts did come,
my nipples point down as if frowning,

as if disappointed by the small mounds
they crown. They were born to stare straight
at the ground, warning new blossoms.

II.

My Father's Fat Back

is my grandmother's back: longer, wide-shouldered, with hair. For the first time in years, I watch him stand naked in front of the dresser—his skin is blue-translucent, almost delicate despite the moles. I notice his body clump in strange places—hunched and aging—held up by spindly legs. And when I see the bulges sink down the sides of his ribcage, I feel sorry for all he tries to hide under good suits and expensive watches, cash stashed in coat pockets from blackjack and craps. I hear his mother screaming in the police station hurling a hairbrush at his fat, teenaged frame after he raced stolen cars in Mamaroneck. She calls him "Sonny Boy." He wishes her dead.

The Savior

I was born to save my father from going to war:
thickets, bamboo, damp heat—I kept him at home.
The war I saved him from lived in our house,

hard ground filled with traps, bad floods,
an enemy that shifted and dodged. Every time
my father threw a dish or a glass or a platter of meat,

I saw the mess on our floor as remains of a battle;
my mother, as nurse, who tended the hurt—
swept up the china and chose what to salvage.

The fights they survived made me press my ears closed.
I'd sit in the tub with shampoo in my hair,
run the faucet to drown out their screaming.

The child who died before me bled out of my mother
in clots, a wound in a rice paddy. The blood stained
my parents' wedding sheets: fine linen soaked in dead cells.

No one cried from what died inside her. But when
they made me, somehow I knew I would have to be perfect:
save my father from war, save my mother from feeling

unloved by the man who begged for me each night
they made love in their one-room apartment on Bleecker Street.
Years later, in college, I walked Bleecker's long blocks,

retraced their steps—young lovers with grocery bags
and decades ahead rolled out like dough to be shaped
and made sweet, to be baked in the oven, waft through the house.

At first, I felt this potential for goodness. I willed myself
to make it through, stayed solid in my mother's womb
like onyx, refused to stain sheets and fail them.

But when he entered her at night, I felt pushed and shoved,
held my breath for all of us, knowing I'd be born to protect
my mother from harm. Love her gently. If I had bled out

of my mother in red silky ribbons, would they have kept trying?
And for how long would her womb keep a place
for the weak unborn? If my father had fought in Vietnam,

would he have learned the fragility of children?
How easy it is to ruin a family with one simple shot?
If I hadn't been born, I wonder, who would my father have hurt?

Girls Who Tend

to their mothers' heartbreaks
before they know their own
suffer more slowly. Sniffling
in bedrooms, these mothers
need daughters, cling to them
like lint, join them in sleep
when the men leave. Like lovers

in rainstorms, they keep quiet
company: watch movies, make supper,
share space under afghans. But
daughters know they're not rapture,
not rockets, just bodies dreaming
of better men, too. They want
as much as their mothers do.

Mixed Doubles

We begged them not to play.
We didn't want to watch them
get beaten by the Hellburns
or Feldsteins or Rosenblooms
as valets lined the parking lot
with Mercedes. My father
slapped at each ball, lopped
at the volleys, wobbled
on girlish ankles too thin
for his weight. He liked to hiss
at bad calls, curse a good serve,
dig his racket down into the clay.
And when he ordered our mother
around the court, we watched her
run like a squirrel on a nut-chase,
frilly lace on her tennis panties
sticking out from under her skirt
like a muted, cut-off bridal train.

Hook

My father paid me to watch
television beside him in bed.

We'd both lay on our backs—
heads supported by pillows—

numbed by the flickering screen.
"Quality Time," he'd say

and he wanted it, gave me
twenty bucks for a Met game,

ten for *Columbo*, five for
fifteen minutes of anything

when I didn't feel like it
and was rushed. Even then

he knew I hated television,
the first thing he touched

when he'd come home from work.
He'd press the chunky metal

buttons of those early remotes
with his crippled index finger,

the same hook he used to pluck
wrinkled bills from his wallet.

Family Dinner

Always, the lamb chops
caught fire, fast flames
rolling out from the broiler.

My mother, skilled in fanning
the fat gusts, still looked scared—
oven mitts pointless, scorched

to brown thread and black dust—
that somehow this blaze, these chops
would be the ones to end it all:

no more cutting
the rib's rare eye out
for me to eat in my high chair

beside the creamed spinach—
green bag boiled and slit—
while my father sucked grease

from the lamb bones alone
with the television, then sped
down the hill in his silver

Corvette to some meeting,
a fire or funeral, some woman
calling his name in distress.

New Year's Party

They swapped wives in my bedroom,
rolled joints in the den,
tried hard to be friendly,
were out of our ken.

My sister would cup
her small ear to the wall
to listen for retching,
for flushing, a fall.

We counted their heaving
like sheep before sleep.
We relished these parties—
our secrets to keep.

At midnight, my father
would pass around hats,
blow noisemakers, toast;
we petted our cats.

Clams Casino were scattered
on fancy blue dishes.
For weeks we found clam shells
and counted our riches.

Born Girl

Two mouths, they'd say
in China, where they'd dump us
in rivers hoping for kings.

Two breasts, they want
in every country, no matter
the luck it took to find the lump.

Two times to be owned—
by father, by husband,
mouths covered or kissed,

breasts flaunted or missed,
lips painted, nails polished,
blood shared or blood spilled

to make daughters like this.

A Family Romance

1.
In my favorite picture,
I lay on my father's bare chest,

five days new to the world,
my body the length of his lungs.

It is afternoon; we are napping;
the pink terrycloth of my stretch suit

the only thing between us.
I don't know when it changed,

when I worried every time
he got a knife to slice tomatoes.

2.
In high school, I found Andrew—
a dancer, so graceful, he shimmered
through space. Sometimes wishing

he were a different kind of boy,
he found himself drawn less to me,
more to men like my father.

Did I know Andrew's lust
in the dark of strange rooms,
all those late nights in Chelsea

when he'd disappear? Did he want
to get sick like the rest of our friends,
join them in some kind of mercy?

I took what he gave me, loved
how I could. He was my mirror;
we both asked for nothing.

3.
Last summer, my father sat drunk
in a restaurant, slurred his last order
of cognac. Still, I complied,

slunk into his Porsche, slammed
the door shut in the August
night-mist. And though I knew

he could kill me, I strapped
myself in. Said nothing.
Like when I made love

to Andrew—his sad penis
tried to find a home in me,
and I let him in every time.

Why I'm Afraid of My Father

When I was small,
my father held my sister
up to the garage door
and shook her to stop
her from crying.

I don't remember
this night but still
I see her tiny face—
splotchy and curious
from being born,

blue eyes shiny, round
as pinballs, lashes long
and fluttery. I see her
mouth startled into quiet,
her back pressed up

against the shingles,
her baby legs dangling
in a stretch suit, his hands
around her ribcage as if
he might love her.

Grey Goose on the Rocks

This purity has taken him years.
No more light rum and Coke,

no more silky Merlot, no scotch,
no martinis at lunch. No sugar,

no color, no olive, no fruit.
Nothing but liquid,

clear as a stream,
mud carp invisible,

eating away at the dirt
on the dark, rank bottom.

What a Daughter Will Do

The thick scar that runs
from the mother's navel
to her pubic bone
is all you need to see
to know what a daughter
will do, how she'll
slice you in half
just to breathe by herself,
then take what's hers
without asking.

Shell

Mottled rust, ring after ring to its milky tower—to think that a creature lived in this cone. Rub it with the thumb, feel it turn like a miniature carousel in a wooden dollhouse, a glass-blown evergreen in a fancy shop window, no memory of what dwelled within. But it's the little hole, midway up, that's disturbing. What stick, what metal shard punctured this shell, maybe killed the small snail in its hole-making? Imagine the leg of the sand crab poking its way into the wall of this shell, looking for love and finding nothing, the home creature farther down or farther up, avoiding the intrusion into its small world. My mother could live in this tower,

this shell, that hole her window to look out past the sea to her daughters who are swimmers, are sailboats, brighter fish, a sparkling school. She makes herself small enough to fit comfortably into the cone, her privacy all she has left now that her girls are full-grown and her husband still a cruel boy in seventh grade who throws rocks at the one girl who likes him the most. Mother wedged in there reading the paper in curlers, the *Times* open on top of the covers. Travel Section. But all I can see are her legs spread wide under her silky nightgown, and I know how glad I am not to have come from that place, but a deep purple scar on her belly. I can't believe she doesn't know how exposed she is to us there on the bed my sister and I love to sleep in when our father's away; we cuddle up in the pink crocheted blanket, get back to that warm place inside her. Looking back,

I imagine we might fit inside this sea shell safe from my father, the porthole our window to know if we'd ever want out of this shell of a home. I imagine us all—my mother, my sister, myself—as a three-headed Rapunzel, too afraid to let our thin, stringy hair down. If that shell were a tower, no one would come save us. We would never be a part of the outside world with such useless hair. This tale is already fragmented, Rapunzel schizophrenic, three voices trapped in one body on the ocean floor. Some kingdom.

III.

First Audition

It was an open call
for *Merrily We Roll Along,*
and I wore a charcoal suit,
blue ribbon in my hair.
Like 900 other teenagers,
I huddled on the floor
next to my instrument,
silent on cheap carpet.

I did my Biology—
committed cell structure to memory—
and tried to make eye contact
with the older boy
strumming his guitar
next to the broken elevator.

When my number was called,
my throat dried out
and I tripped into the studio.
The judges smiled vaguely
from their corner
where everything happened.
There was the accompanist, of course,
and a smoking panel of adults who sifted
through stacks of headshots,
separated us into mysterious piles.

Stephen Sondheim was there, too,
but I was too young at 14
to recognize him or to know
what someone like that
could do for me. He was the first
in a series of important people
to watch me and my worn sheet music:
the little girl in her mother's shoes,
who forgot the words of her song
and hated the piano player.

Dance Recital

No tutus, no bake sales,
no parents with flowers.
At 15, I danced in a bar.
I'd hike up my leotards
as men 20 years older
held tight to the necks
of their beer bottles.
I watched their thick fingers
as I found my place—
a faded square on the floor
with an "X" of tape.

This wasn't a stage—
no curtains or wings—
but a dance floor
with colored lights
and a handful of teenaged girls
ready to shimmy and pulse
in the noise, in the smoke-fog.

When I tell this story,
I like to pretend I didn't know
my allure. But I glittered
my lashes and played with my hair.
I knew the prize of my youth
against their wives and girlfriends,
my legs more firm and curious.
I knew I wanted something real
from their slick-lipped gazes, dreamt
about what they could do with me.

I loved that teasing on school nights
while other kids were in bed.
I loved that last step
into the employee bathroom,
before I'd put on my clothes,
wipe lipstick off on my sleeve,
and return to my Geometry proofs.

Chorus Boys

Before I hurt my back, I'd meet them for dinner
on matinee days—Wednesdays and Saturdays
when Broadway was thrumming with tourists.

I greeted them with kisses at the stage door,
while other girls waited for autographs,
their *Playbills* opened like teenage vaginas.

My chorus boys didn't want out-of-town girls;
they wanted me to talk to between shows,
eat Thai food near the Majestic, the Winter Garden,

the Ambassador. When we crossed 8th Avenue,
I wanted people to see me latched on to these stars,
these lean men with show jackets flashing

behind us like money. I listened closely
to their tales from the wings, their missed cues
and flat notes, sprained ankles which waited

til after the show. They asked about class
where I spent my days—pointing and flexing,
kicking and spinning, throwing my body around

because I thought it would never break.
And when it did, under hot lights at a screen test,
I knew that I didn't want Hollywood.

I wanted New York and a show jacket
and my name in a *Playbill* near the long list
of chorus boys who didn't scare me

like other men, who held my hands soft,
kept their tongues to themselves.

First Boyfriend

I still wear his Levi's
with the patched crotch—
a tattered maze
of striped fabric in my groin.
I begged for them
before he left for college,
before he dated men.
"I always want to be
in your pants," I joked.
And we both laughed,
knowing that in the fall
all I'd have left of him
was a torn back pocket
that hung like a flap of sky.

Paris at 20

Alone, I went to museums and drank coffee,
ate chocolate crêpes for breakfast, and hoped
that a man would come show me the world.

On the Metro, I found Jean-Charles—
handsome and dangerous, wrapped tight
in his blue jeans—and followed him

along the Seine, where we drank wine all night,
my French quickening with every sip.
We held hands in the rain and ran fast—

drunk and wet—six flights up to his flat,
a dark room with a fire and floor pillows
made for taking off clothes. At first,

it felt good, and I wanted him—wanted it—
until I didn't. My bra wrapped around my neck,
my underwear waded around my ankles,

and I wanted out of his arms, of that flat,
maybe even Paris. I tried to struggle free,
to tell him "no," but Jean-Charles didn't

understand the urgency of my English:
"Quoi, Quoi?" he kept asking, "Quoi, Quoi?"
He breathed French vowels into my breasts,

pressed his thumbs in my back—an explorer
thirsty for foreign land. How could he know
what was wrong if I didn't? How could he

know I needed a taxi back to Le Marais,
to an old flame, now a drag queen doing cabaret
at La Cage Aux Folles—baubles, feathers,

lip-synching in French—who, with his head
in a wig cap, offered the safety of American
arms, late at night in Gay Paris.

Hunger

After the lunch shift, I hid
in the restroom or went down
to the dock to suck what was left
of a lobster claw, use my teeth
on a crab leg, pull a mussel
from its blue-ringed shell.

In the bus station, next to trays
of dirty glasses, I kept my own
butter—drawn and golden—to dip
the fried fish I found, snack in secret
between the ketchup and the steak knives.
I didn't care who had been there

before me, whose scaly hands
or bloody gums had made their mark
on what I thought to be a perk
for all those hours I scraped cole slaw
into a trash heap, wiped beer
from old barstools where people left

razor clams and napkins streaked
by tartar sauce. They didn't know
I took their oysters and shrimp
into my mouth like new lovers,
wrapped their leftovers under my shirt
to bring down to the shore. At dusk—

no thought of the lemon wedges I forgot,
the coffee that came too late, the lost
stained check—I listened to the lapping
of The Sound, felt the shrunken eye
of the sun, watched the pink trace of light
disappear above the ocean's lip.

Farmers Market

We both sample blood oranges,
but buy avocados instead.
I pay with a five; he fumbles
through his wallet dropping coins
into the box of lemons.

I think he is homeless,
but then I notice his hands—
just like John's hands—
dry and jaundiced, choosing fruit.
His khakis hang loose
like drapes in an old motel,
and I can't help but follow his feet
as he walks toward the artichokes.

The last summer I saw John
at the Union Square Market,
he carried a flat of strawberries,
which he planned to dip in chocolate.
He was still able to smile then—
a big one next to the cherries—
holding hydrangeas in newspaper
for his railroad apartment in Brooklyn.

And though I knew he was sick—
scarves wrapped his neck in July—
I never thought he would die.
Not then. Not the way he darted
around the market with his mouth open
at the joy of summer corn,
the yellow and white calico of it.

Five Years After John's Death

Tree roots scar the yard,
break through the dirt

like old fingers.
A vast reach, the mingling

of the below ground
and the above. How held

I still am by what turns
to dust beneath us—

breastbone, seedling.

Teaching High School

It's not the work I mind,
just how I have to beg.
Every day a rude dance:
training chimps or seals
to peel fruit or balance globes
on their greasy, pimpled noses.

Ruben

In the Boys' Room of the Catholic School,
you pissed your name on new tile
as the priest washed his hands.
Later, told not to wear makeup
for the yearbook picture, you protested.
Lost. Came to me with a poem.

I saw you today—years later—
outside The Gap. Gone the spiked hair,
pale face, black lips, deep maroon lines
around the eyes. Just a smile of relief
to be done with high school, new ring
in your lip shining in noon light.

I was glad to see you, but forgot your name.
I remembered everything else (the slouch
in the desk chair, your notebook wrinkled
like an old shirt, safety pins thrust through
red combat boots), but I could not call you
by name and I felt bad, like you knew

you were just one of the herd, after all.
And it is only now—as I sit at the airport
eating my grilled cheese sandwich—
that it comes to me: *Ruben. Ruben.*
The pierced ring still a small way to be
recognized, a small way to be different.

The Girl Who Hanged Herself

And when I think of her legs dangling
in stiff blue jeans, her snapped neck,

and her body limp over the bathtub,
I think of her digging her name

into the school's scuffed furniture,
how all I knew of this girl was that scratch,

the fine-lined, heart-shaped tattoo on her breast
and the way she waved goodbye to her friends

in the hallway as I stood at the blackboard,
brushing chalk dust off my skirt.

J-O-B

I eat no food
in my classroom.

I clutch my coat.
I hold my bladder.

At home, I settle in
with tea and buttered toast,

let the hair slip out
of its tight band.

I wear no bra.
I write my poem.

IV.

Attached

When I moved from New York to California,
I thought I could wear a sundress every night.

I refused to buy sweaters and shivered,
my words slurred by my chattering teeth.

Men gave me their jackets in movie theaters,
and I never rolled up the sleeves. I wanted

to feel their largeness on me, see my body
get lost in the heat. Now, my favorite sweater

is my father's: a ropy cotton, shapeless
where it hangs near my knees.

One Passover at the fourth cup of wine
he started to sweat, then pulled it over his head

and jammed it in my lap. "Hold this," he said,
and rushed through the story of the plagues.

My father is always hot. As a little girl,
I noticed underarm stains on his polo shirts,

tweed jackets with patches soaked-through.
At night, my sister and I listened to the arc of piss

through the bathroom door to know how much
he had to drink and how scared we should be.

Before passing out, he'd yell for one of us
to get him ice water or turn up the air.

I was always too cold. I wore his sweatpants
to sleep at night, and rubbed my feet together,

hoping to start a fire.

Anza-Borrego

That night, the desert,
the silver sand's expanse
made bigger by our being

lost, stuck in my hatchback,
that poor car spinning its old wheels
in a ditch back-lit by stars

and lush planets, visible
as our naked limbs
in the creosote dusk.

I was 21, spent from the city,
night's peach-tinted sunrise
a gift wrapped in tissue. And you—

your chipped front tooth,
the Badlands' glare—
our future dangled in dry air.

A Good Day

All of a sudden it hits you:
you have enough money,
the weather is warm,
and your favorite song—
the one you haven't heard in years—
plays on the car radio,
and you still know all the words,
and you hit the rough high note,
and you hold it for as long
as it needs to be held.
Then you come home,
and you dance around your apartment,
and you don't mind being alone,
or that you can't remember
the last time you danced
not alone in your apartment,
and you used to be a dancer.
But your lover—who's still
at work—loves you, and you know
when he comes home
he will kiss you hello,
and eat your linguine,
and you'll have a glass of wine,
and watch TV on the couch,
or maybe read a magazine,
and know that some days
are better than others,
and this one, better than most.

My Boyfriend's Mother Calls

and I worry she will suck him back in,
lure him to float in her waters, skin

and worlds beyond me. Preverbal.
He does not know any of this—

that he's in and I'm out,
that her phone call is a charged chord

that rings dissonant in my ears
and echoes through our hallway like a dirge.

What does she want from him now
after making him? And making him

husband, father, brother, lover—every man
who ever left. But faithful. Therefore better.

And when I think of him at 16
dragging his own father down the stairs—

passed out again, head banging
on the banister—I think of him

in utero, no choice
but to breathe in her smoke.

Engagement Ring

I wanted something old.
It isn't enough

that diamonds are mined,
dug up from the earth's crust;

that platinum is elemental.
I wanted something someone

wore for life and died in,
defects a part of its history.

First Meal, Married; Dinner, Oia

The fish arrives intact
on a stark white platter,

charred, but slick in its oils.
The blistered skin

still bubbles as it did
on the grill grates, filling

sea air with fish-smoke.
I suck at its ivory ribs,

lick the bits along the spine,
then the fanned, glistening

tail, delicate cheeks, all meat
but the unknown gland

and stiff eyeballs stuck in its
burnt head, facing me off

from its fortress of bone,
mourning its skeleton.

What Was

The Pantheon was once a fish market.
Christianity, a small cult.

My husband was once just a lover
I met on vacation, dancing on sawdust.

Now, with his mother's gait,
he backs away, adjusts the shutter,

flashes against the ruins
of the Roman Forum. This picture

will also be a relic—grandchildren
struck by my unweathered face.

Old Poems You Wish You Hadn't Written

Naked Verses arrived today,
an old poem of mine inside.

I reddened with shame, refused
to read, sneered at nude photos

of fat women grilling hot dogs,
ragged children tossing frisbees,

two old men playing tennis
in sun hats and sneakers,

their withered cocks staring at me
like two awful sunken eyes.

Faithful Wife, Reading Ovid

If I were Juno,
I'd have already made
a barnyard of animals
from all the nymphs
my god had fucked:
the waitress, a heifer;
the writer, a camel;
the dancer, a blind swan,
doomed to float on a lake
until her neck skin wrinkled,
and her feathers lost sheen.
I'd let her eyesight return
when things had gone far enough.
For years until death,
I'd make her look down
at the water, see herself
weathered as a seawall,
clear as Narcissus' reflection.

Invisible

What I do everyday
is invisible.

I rinse coffee mugs.
Stack newspapers.

Hang towels.
Change linen.

Replenish the ice.
Ask me now

how my mother
spent her days.

Childless

In the Middle Ages,
pregnant women wishing
for beautiful children
were to look at beautiful things:
handmade lace, just-cut emeralds,
painted cherubs floating on canvas,
reaching past the gilded frame.

Empty, I just glare
at potted plants, play with the dent
of my mother's gold locket,
consider those things with surprises
inside—firearms, coconuts,
antique music boxes with rusty springs.

Sometimes, I think I should
stick with growing things:
the avocado pit sprouting leaves
in its tooth-picked house,
bags of seed, crocus bulbs
snug in their slow hibernation.

Or, I could a keep a live snail,
finger its shell to feel the slime
contracting in fear, study
the desert tortoise burrowing
inside its mud-dried home.

Instead, I dig into sandboxes,
looking for deep-buried shovels,
a lost earring, stone.

Contemplating Motherhood: Hope, Alaska

Spawned-out salmon
float in green water.
Their scales are yellow,
their eyes plucked out
like raisins. Gone
the leaping Coho,
King, and Dolly Varden:
no more thrash
through the current;
no more dodging
the bear-mouth.
This is August:
sleek fish eggless,
senseless, snaggle-toothed,
gray. The murky ground
an empty nursery.

The Affair

All the eyes of Argus
wouldn't have helped me.

What there was to see, I ignored.
And what I could not see,
I was glad for, relieved.

I might as well have been
that head chopped off,
that mind rolling down the hill

to its death, eyes as stars
spread out across the night sky.

V.

Reading James Wright

The world is loud.
Hunger settles in the body

like silt, like sludge. I sit
for lunch and open my book—

his earth-born quiet fills me
as I fill my mouth, taste wasabi,

pickled ginger, sliced fish
and sticky rice. No one can ruin

this pleasure, this salvage.

Reading Roethke

Sap and loam. Root and weed.
The underbelly of your yearning

rises to the surface like sulfur.
Its stink is what you love

and can't endure—its mulch
and rot; its pure dark rank

unfurling. I think of you
ordering a piece of raw steak—

tearing at its sinew with your teeth.
How can I sink into flesh like that?

How can I join the animal world?
The kingdom of plants?

Volcanic ash, broken shells,
the crusty, muddied earth?

Reading Akhmatova

The Bear-Witness Poets
make me feel useless.

What have I seen?
There were no labor camps

in Fairfield County.
No breadlines

on Christopher Street.
I do not have a son—

taken and pummeled,
lost in a brutal regime.

What I witnessed
happened behind

painted white shingles
and navy blue shutters,

rope-patterned wallpaper
in an oak-filled dining room

where people rarely ate,
nor lit the candles

standing upright
in their silver.

Touch Has a Memory

-John Keats

It remembers the first
uncertain flutters,
the starlings in the stomach,
the first boy who—
on your startled upper arm—
made spirals with his fingers
and then went away to boarding school,
left you with those patterned loops
to conjure up on bike rides or in gym class
or when shopping for bras with your mother.
You'd squint your eyes to bring it on,
memory: solid as a horse,
tender as a scar, and somehow
writ in water.

Reading Ovid

I would also like to be transformed—

bones softened to pond water,
skin spread into lily pads,
hair green, a tangle of weeds.

The wrinkles on the water
would show all the life inside me,
the croak of a bullfrog

relief from all.

Acknowledgments

Thank you to the editors of the following publications in which some of these poems (or earlier versions of them) first appeared (or will soon appear):

Alaska Quarterly Review: "Babysitting"
Ariel's Dream: "Reading Ovid," "Touch Has a Memory"
Connecticut River Review: "Farmers Market," "Five Years After John's Death," "What Was"
The Dillydoun Review: "Paris at 20"
Exit 7: "A Family Romance"
5 AM: "First Boyfriend"
Flyway: "Dance Recital"
Georgetown Review: "Miss Southern Connecticut"
Hour of the Pearl: "Attached," "Reading Roethke"
Limestone: "Invisible"
New York Quarterly: "First Audition"
Poetry East: "Engagement Ring"
River Styx: "Faithful Wife, Reading Ovid"
Smoky Blue Literary and Arts Magazine: "Anza-Borrego"
Tidal Journal: "Hunger" (First Place Winner of the 2018 Myra Shapiro Prize for Poetry, sponsored by the International Women's Writing Guild)
William and Mary Review: "What a Daughter Will Do"

"Mixed Doubles" and "The Girl Who Hanged Herself" were included in *Changing Harm to Harmony: The Bullies and Bystanders Project* (Marin Poetry Center Press, 2015).

This book contains long-ago-written poems that never would have been ushered into the world without the encouragement and support of so many people—young, old, near, far, alive, and dead.

Thank you to my mother, Judy Milwe, for giving me this life.

Deepest gratitude to Naomi Lieberman for putting me on this path (in the last century!), and to Jack Grapes, my first—and still fabulous—writing teacher.

Heartfelt thanks to several important teachers and mentors along the way: Sharon Olds and Ellen Bass at Esalen; David Ulin, through PEN West, in my Santa Monica High School classroom; Jane Hirshfield, Thomas Sayers Ellis, and two late greats—Liam Rector and Jason Shinder—at the Bennington Writing Seminars; Alexander Weinstein, Amelia Martens, and Britton Shirley at the Martha's Vineyard Institute of Creative Writing.

I am indebted to some key readers who offered wisdom and incisive feedback when words were hard to come by: Kate Egan, Claire North, Julia Rosenblum, and Rob Wilder.

Thank you, Kwame Dawes, for your time in offering much-needed critical insight at the eleventh hour.

Great appreciation for countless friends and colleagues who have supported me in the Santa Monica-Malibu Unified School District where I have worked for three decades:
-Carol Jago, thank you for hiring me and trusting me so early on.
-Sylvia Rousseau and Eva Mayoral, thank you for being true visionary leaders and including me in your vision.
-Catherine Baxter, thank you for always supporting me and our family since my very first day of work.
-Jessica Garrido, your unwavering and compassionate guidance kept me going this year, truly.
-Sarah Blitz, I could not do it without you. And I would not want to.
-JAMS Family—especially Amy Beeman-Solano, Hanna Duff, and Steve Richardson. You take me as I am, and I know it is not always easy. You are so loved and appreciated.

Thank you to Joan and Jessica for always being in (and on) my corner, literally and figuratively.

Thank you to photographer extraordinaire, Gene Reed, for making me look good again.

Thanks also to Cortés Alexander for almost 40 years of haircuts, hilarity, and unconditional love.

I don't have strong enough words to express the feelings I hold in my heart for my dear old friends: Andrew Currie, Johnny Anzalone, and my long-dead John Aller. Neither my life nor these poems would be the same without these beautiful men—all the laughter and all the memories.

I love you forever, Carol Seder.

Thank you to my brilliant and beloved Whitney Scott for the use of her stunning photograph on the cover, among so many other things.

I won the jackpot to share blood with some of the most fierce and loving women on the planet: my sister, Alison Milwe Grace; my aunt, Liz Milwe; and my cousin, Merri Milwe. Life is so much better with you in it.

Uncle Peter, I miss you. Cousin Timmy, same.

34 years of true love and deep gratitude to my husband, Tom, who always believes in me even when I don't believe in myself.

This book is dedicated to our children: Tupelo, Jersey, and Walden. You are all my favorites.

Cindy Milwe was born and raised in Westport, Connecticut and now lives in Venice, California. She earned her BA from NYU's Gallatin Division, her MA in English Education from Columbia University's Teachers College, and her MFA in Poetry from Bennington College. She has worked for three decades in the Santa Monica-Malibu Unified School District as an English teacher, yoga teacher, poetry workshop facilitator, writing interventionist, literacy coach, and instructional coach. In the last 30 years, her poems have been published in numerous journals, magazines, and anthologies, and she has received several awards, including the Parent/Writer Fellowship at the Martha's Vineyard Institute of Creative Writing for her poem, "Legacy," the Myra Shapiro Prize for Poetry for her poem, "Hunger," and a Pushcart Prize nomination for her poem, "Memorial." This is her first book.